The Book Of Golf Tips

We have helped 1,000's of golfers,
Let us help you !

Over 400 golf tips including:

Eliminate that slice
Pro's secrets to good tee shots
Pro's secrets to good putting
Getting out of trouble includes:
Trees
Sand
Water
Ruff
Hazards
Playing smart golf
Exercises & Warm ups
Course management (finesse golf)
What club to use (yardage)
Secrets of the game
Golf Equipment
Rules of golf
Golf Etiquette
Proper golf attire

THE BOOK OF GOLF TIPS

Written for beginning golfers and
Those struggling with their game

1) Keep your head down

2) Swing Easy

3) Enjoy

Copyright © 2014
New and Updated Edition
By Carey Erichson
Pioneer, CA 95666
800-717-4633

THE BOOK OF GOLF TIPS

My Handicap Is How Low ???

TABLE OF CONTENTS

Preface
Learning the game of golf
Secrets of the game
Golf Terminology
Addressing the ball
Success with the driver
Eliminate the slice
Push and pulled shots
The shank
The art of putting
Getting out of trouble
Course Management
Golf equipment
Rules of golf
Golf etiquette
Proper golf attire
Golfers with disabilities
Golfing for juniors
A little golf humor
How to buy and clean used clubs
Summary of golf shots
Club yardage charts
Other books by author

PREFACE

I have been playing golf for over **70** years. That's a long time in anyone's book. I was never a great golfer, but I did OK throughout the years. I couldn't hit the long ball, but I always hit it straight. This drove my opponents crazy.

The one thing I learned over the years is that there are only two ways to improve your golf game. Work on the basics and practice.

Most golfers **today** depend more on new equipment than they do on the basics.

Without a doubt, the new equipment is more forgiving and helps you hit the ball farther. My question to you is, farther where? Into the trees or out of bounds?

If you can't hit the ball straight to begin with, then how can new equipment help you? I have yet to see a golfer, with a bad slice, straighten their ball out by just buying new equipment. The best putter made will not put the ball in the hole. **YOU** still have to do it.

There are a lot of secrets in the game of golf. I have tried to include as many as I could in this book. We also discuss course management.

Over the years my golf game has slipped quite a bit. My shots are getting shorter, my body hurts more and sometimes golf has become a chore instead of a pleasure.

What is my answer to all of this? Practice the basics and concentrate on **my short** game. If I improve my short game, I can possibly pick up a stroke that I have lost in distance.

With all of this in my mind I have decided to go back to the basics. This book is being written as I am going through my own training program. This way I can share my knowledge and experience with the millions of other **Happy Golfers.**

LEARNING THE GAME OF GOLF

Before we get into any kind of instruction on golf we should have a good understanding of what good instruction consists of and how it should be applied to beginning golfers.

There are two types of professionals in the golfing world. One is a professional golfer and the other a golfing professional.

A professional golfer is one who makes his living by playing in tournaments and living off of his winnings, plus other income. They travel extensively.

A golf professional can also participate in professional tournaments, but his living is made in teaching and his office is basically the local club. Travel is at a minimum.

A golf professional makes most of his money from golf instruction plus a percentage of sales from the pro shop merchandise. The two professional classifications are really quite different.

Why is this important to know? The club house pro is a better teacher than the touring pro. The touring pro can only worry about his game and no other. My guess is that the greatest players we know could not teach a good game of golf. Don't hold me to this quote, but that is what they tell me.

There is a real knack to teaching of any kind. It is a step by step process that if presented correctly will have great benefits for the students. If the teacher takes shortcuts, and a lot of them do, then the students will suffer.

Now, on the other hand, if the student takes shortcuts, they will suffer even more because they did not learn correctly from the start. This is where most new golfers are today. All they hear about is new equipment and how it will improve their game. They forget that you have to know the basics of the golf swing before you can advance to the next step towards good golf.

When I was being certified to teach junior bowlers I learned one of the most important lessons in my life and I have carried that into my later years with great satisfaction and even a little success.

At the very end of our certification, the instructor asked us to take our bowling balls out on to the lanes so we could bowl. Next he said he wanted all right hand bowlers on a certain set of lanes and all left hand bowlers on another.

Then he told the right handers to bowl left handed and the left handers to bowl right handed. Well, he had a real zoo out there on the bowling lanes. In a short period of time and before we hurt ourselves, he told us to stop.

"Now", he said, "you know how your beginning students feel and don't ever forget it". "If you do, you will never be a good instructor".

There are a lot of good golf instructors out there and to find one will take some time. I would recommend asking a friend for a referral and go to that instructor, even if you have to drive some distance.

I also recommend that men go to a male instructor and ladies go to a female instructor. The male and female bodies are completely different. For the gals, it is especially important that the instructor understands the body structure and what physical conditions may exist and how to get around them.

Last, but not least, we need to look at the approach the instructor takes in teaching you the game. Some believe in teaching the basics while others are into advance performance and modern technology.

I believe in learning the **basics of golf** and understanding the game. When you feel like your game is to a point that's ready for the next level, go into the advanced technology, if you can comprehend it.

Advanced technology will not help you learn the basics of the game. It is designed to help you get those extra yards from your existing game.

When learning the game of golf, take the time to understand the basics and then **practice** what you have learned.

Our book is written in a manner that will not confuse you. Our tips are short and to the point. We do not have long drawn out explanations that will lose you after a few sentences.

SECRETS OF THE GAME

PHYSICAL AWARENESS

Always adapt the game to your body. Never try and adapt your body to the game. The average instructor will try and make your body do what is needed to play the game. An excellent instructor will teach you the game to fit your body.

Age and physical limitations, within every one of us, vary to a great degree. We can not all play the same game.

When we are young and limber, our bodies can do just about anything. We hit long shots, mostly off the fairways, but it's long. The same young players can't chip or putt. They are too hung up on distance.

When we get older and mature, we hit the ball a shorter distance, but straighter. We also learn to practice our chipping and putting to save a stroke on each hole to make up for the loss in distance.

WARMING UP

It is very important to go through a series of stretching exercises before you play a round of golf. The golf swing requires our body to bend and twist in a very unconventional way.

I assume everyone wakes up in the morning with some stiff muscles. I know that I do and it takes awhile to loosen up the old body.

Stretching exercises will help relieve tension. They will also help your body relax so the golf swing will not cause you any discomfort as you play your round of golf.

There are many stretching exercises, but the ones that will do you the most good are those that turn your body from straight ahead to ¾ around to the back. This simulates the back swing. Moving your arms up and down and from side to back helps loosen up the shoulders. Bend overs are excellent, especially if you have an oversize tummy. This exercise will stretch your back and help eliminate back problems.

These exercises can be done in the privacy of your home. The next series should be done at the golf course.

Hitting a bucket of golf balls on the practice range is not a good idea for most people. The reason being that you will hit the golf ball enough times throughout the day. If you hit a bucket of balls, your body will be tired before you even tee off. Here is a better way.

Get out a seven iron and take about 15 easy swings. Don't just swing the club, but put some thought behind each swing. Next take out the driver or #3 wood and do the same thing.

This very simple series of exercises puts your body into the **golf swing mood**. You are slowly working your way into your golf game, mentally and physically. It doesn't take much to warm up if you do it properly.

PRACTICE

The secret to any sport is practice. The problem we face here is discipline. When we go to the driving range we find ourselves hitting the bucket of balls with no plan in mind. We think our hitting the bucket will loosen us up and we are ready to hit the course. Actually, all we did was waste our time and energy.

Time on the driving range should be used wisely and with a definite routine. Most pros will tell you to warm up with your favorite club, say around a 7 or 9 iron. From there you work your way down to the driver. By the time you get down to the driver your body is relaxed and ready for the power club.

When practicing, use the clubs that give you the most trouble. Don't waste time hitting clubs that you have mastered.

The practice tee should be used for improving your swing, **not** for hitting golf balls. The ball is there so you will have something to connect with at the end of your swing.

Take the practice tee time to work on your swing tempo and full body turn. Without these two factors you have no golf game. Where the ball goes is of no importance at this time. While you are working on your swing tempo and turn, you will notice the ball is going straighter and farther automatically. If the ball doesn't do this then you are most likely practicing wrong and need to make changes. Remember that **change is inevitable,** not only in sports, but every phase of our lives.

THE GOOD SAMARITANS

We all have friends who want to help us. In golf and other sports everyone wants to help. By doing this they are making themselves look and feel important whether or not they know what they're talking about and **most of them don't.**

Anyone can see that a person is lifting their head or swinging too fast. These comments are very helpful and can improve your game. When it comes to the swing and proper club position, watch out for the know-it-all golfer. They will have you upside down in no time at all.

When you find someone who can help your game and you enjoy their comments, stick with them. You don't need to hear that you are doing something dumb, you already know that. What you want to know is how is the problem corrected. It may take awhile to correct the swing, but at least you are headed in the right direction.

Another thing to remember is that when you are making changes, you will most likely get **worse** before you improve. This is very discouraging and will have a great mental effect on you. Be patient and look for improvement. When you see signs that your game is changing, give yourself time to work on the problems. They will not go away quickly.

SCORING

When you are taking golf lessons or working on your game, **DO NOT KEEP SCORE**. When you play golf it should be to work on your golf swing, not to record a score. When you are a member of a golf club you are required to turn in your playing cards. So, do not play competitive golf. Go out on the course and practice. Hit three or four balls whenever possible and work on the problem areas. Score is the last thing that should be considered. Once you have hit **more than** one ball on the same fairway, your score is not legal and can't be turned in.

THE SWING

Now we are in the area that baffles all of us. What is a proper swing and how do we maintain it? This can not be learned from a book. Sometimes videos can help us get on the right track but, I really believe a pro should come in and with their expertise, get you in the right swing tempo for your game.

Due to the variety of physical conditions, each player will have a different swing tempo and follow through.

One thing we can agree on is that the swing tempo will be just about the same for all clubs in your bag.

The club length and angle of the club face will make the ball go farther in some cases and higher in others.

This is the basic fact that is taught to all beginning golfers. As you develop your game, the swing tempo may vary depending upon your level of competence. Good golfers will vary their swing tempo to get the ball to do **their** thing, what ever it may be.

One thing to remember, right from the beginning, is that swinging harder and faster will not make the ball go farther. In most cases it will make the ball do the opposite. When you **over power** the ball it will react in a **negative** manner.

Just for the fun of it, the next time you are on the practice tee try this little routine. Hit the first 1/3 bucket of balls with your normal swing. Then hit the next 1/3 of the bucket with just a half swing. You will be amazed at how far and straight the half swing will send your ball. Why? Because you will be back within your good **swing tempo** with the half swing.

Most golfers will not do this because you look like an idiot not taking that big powerful back swing. We are creatures of habit and until we change our habits nothing else will change.

One of my very favorite quotations is the following:
(I do not know where it came from)

> "You will keep on getting
> what you have been getting,
> If you keep on doing what
> you have been doing"

SOME GOLF TERMINOLOGY

GRIP Hold the club firmly with the last 3 fingers on your left hand. Use the right hand more to guide the club shaft. **Do not** squeeze the golf club tightly. There should be no tension in your arms or wrists. The V between your fingers and thumbs, on both hands, should point to the right shoulder.

STANCE Square stance has **both** feet parallel to the line of target.

the Open stance has the **left** foot back of line parallel to the target.

Closed stance has **right** foot back of the line parallel to the target.

WEIGHT Weight will always be on the **left** side except on tee shots. On tee shots you will place your weight on the **right** side. The reason for this is that on fairway shots you hit **down** on the ball. On tee shots you hit **up** on the ball.

TAKE A WAY

Your back swing should start low and slow along the ground. Do not pick the club head up. Let the club leave the ground as you start your back turn.

FACE Refers to the angle of the club face surface.

Closed face means club surface is in a straight up and down position.

Open face means club surface is facing upwards creating loft.

HOOK   Ball flies to the left. (Not Good)

SLICE   Ball flies to the right (Not Good)

DRAW   Ball flies straight and then curves left. Created by partially closed stance. (Excellent)

FADE   Ball flies straight and then curves right.

Created by partially open stance. (Excellent)

WIND

low   When hitting **into** the wind, play for a low trajectory shot using a **longer** club than normal.

high   When hitting **with** the wind, play for a high trajectory shot using a **shorter** club than normal.

TURN

Body turns from the hips up. Head and eyes are almost directly over the ball, maybe a little behind it. Keep left arm stiff. **Do not** bend the left elbow at the top of your back swing.

FOCUS

Always keep your eyes and your thoughts **in front** of the ball. Never think about anything behind the ball.

All movement behind the ball has to become automatic. Any thoughts behind the ball will break your concentration and timing.

Another thought under focus should be to visualize each shot before you take it. This gets you into the mental frame of mind to make an excellent shot.

WAGGLE

A term used to indicate moving the club over or behind the ball. This movement helps the player get the feel of a shot. Used by quite a few of the young players.

Many golfers do not put the club on the ground before they shoot. It is kind of like a waggle, but done to keep your arms in motion without stopping and starting again when addressing the ball.

"FORE"

A term used to warn other players on the course that the ball is hit in their direction and might strike them. This came from an old army infantry slogan "Down in the foreground" as each line of army riflemen took their shot at the enemy during battle. It was later shortened to "Fore"

When you have hit your ball in the direction of other players, yell "Fore" with some authority. If you don't, the other players probably won't hear you and then get mad when the ball comes sailing through.

Getting hit by a golf ball is very painful and can cause some serious injuries.

So --- yell "Fore" very loudly !!

FOLLOW THROUGH (Clubs #1 through #9)

One of the most important aspects of any sport is the follow through. This is especially true in the game of golf. What do we mean by follow through?

After you make contact with the ball, your club face should be aiming right at your target. The club face direction will not change until you make your turn on the upswing. Not only does the club stay in line with your target, but also your body. Your face and chest should be facing the target. This is the turn on the upswing. Between the club face and the turn of your body, you will have completed a full follow through.

Why is this so important? Consistency. You can never **stop** your swing the same way twice. If you have a good follow through, your swing will always stop at the same place. On top of your left shoulder.

When you watch the young pros on television you can't see their extension towards the pin because they swing too fast. Watch the Seniors on TV and you can see the swing like it was in slow motion. Most of them can't throw the club over their left shoulder as fast or as far, so you can easily see their straight out extension to the pin.

FOLLOW THROUGH (Pitching - Chipping)

On the pitch and chip shots you will not take a full back swing or use a full follow through. The reason being these are delicate shots and so close to the green.

Your backswing and follow through will be up to a ¾ swing, but you will still need to follow through. Do not stop your club after contact.

You will need to develop a feel for these shots. Again, practice makes perfect.

FOLLOW THROUGH (Putting)

The theory in putting is completely different than all other shots in golf. When you putt, your body does not move. You keep your head and body steady at all times. The only things that move are your arms. Lock your elbows and wrists to accomplish this.

The follow through in putting comes after you strike the ball. Your left arm is stiff and you hold the club head of the putter in a straight line with your target. You will extend the putter two or three feet towards the target after striking the ball. **Do not stop the momentum of the putter going forward**. Let it stop all by itself. (Just like the golf club when it gets over the left shoulder).

ADDRESSING THE GOLF BALL

Where do we place the golf ball in our stance and how do we address the ball with the club?

First you need to find the "bottom of your swing" for every club in your bag. This is the spot your club first hits the grass on your downswing. I believe this to be the most important element of the golf swing.

For tee shots, place the ball in **front** of the bottom of your swing, so you will be hitting up on the ball. This gives you height and distance. You will also place the majority of your weight on the **right** side.

For fairway shots, position the ball slightly **behind** the bottom of your swing so you will be hitting down on the ball.

Most people don't understand where the divot comes from. You hit the ball first and then the ground. The divot is in front of the ball, not behind it. You are basically popping the ball up into the air on fairway shots. You will place the majority of your weight on the **left** side.

Next we position our feet. The right and left foot should be about shoulder width on the long shots and narrower on shorter shots.

Let's start with the driver and hit the various clubs down the fairway. Since we are going to discuss all of the clubs we will assume we are on a long par five and it will take a few swings to reach the green.

DRIVER

Address the ball so that it is just about even with your left heel. Use a partially closed stance, (right foot back of target line), and place your weight on the **right** side.

Position your hands **behind** the ball. Line the shaft up in the middle of your body. The theory here is to hit the ball on the upswing off of the tee.

This will also apply to all other tee shots no matter which club you use. The position of your hands **behind** the ball is the secret here. Almost all other golf shots will have your hands **in front** of the ball.

FAIRWAY WOODS AND LONG IRONS (2 - 5)

Address the ball so that it is inside your left heel about one inch or so. Use a square stance. Your hands will be **in front** of the ball. The difference between a tee shot and a fairway shot is that you **hit down** on the ball with all fairway shots. To position your hands at the correct angle, place them in the middle of your left thigh as a starting place. From here you can move them an inch or two to the right until you feel a comfortable swing. Your weight will be on your **left** side.

Many golfers have a devil of a time using a 3 wood or long iron on the fairways. This is due to the longer shafts. To offset this problem you can choke up on the club an inch or two and place the ball more in the middle of your body stance. For some reason this works for many golfers.

MEDIUM/SHORT IRON SHOTS (6 - 8)

You will address these iron shots the same way you do long iron shots. The only difference is that with each higher numbered club you will move the ball back in your stance about one inch for each club. Your weight will be on your **left** side. You will also narrow your stance a bit.

PITCHING IRONS (9 - WEDGES)

You will address the shot as with all other irons. You will bring your feet closer together and use an open stance. Your back swing will be about ½ **to** ¾ depending upon the yards your ball has to travel. The position of the ball will be inside your right heel. Your weight will be on the **left** side.

Always pitch to land the ball 3 - 6 feet in front of the pin. It will roll the rest of the way.

CHIPPING

Chipping refers to all shots around the green. Your ball will be twelve yards or less from the surface of the green. Here you will hear all kinds of theories on the proper shot.

I personally like to use a seven iron with a putting stroke. The club face angle will get the ball up in the air just enough to clear the tall grass. The putting stroke will get the ball back down on the green quickly so it will roll to the pin. Some of the young pros use a driver for this shot. The driver has a smooth bottom and will not get caught up in the grass as an iron might do. They also use a flop shot and we won't go there.

SIDE HILL LIES

If the ball is above your feet, choke up on the club one or two inches. Use a closed stance and aim to the **right** of your target. There is a normal tendency to hook this shot. Use one club longer than normal and put your weight on the **left** side.

If the ball is below your feet, aim to the **left** of your target as there is a normal tendency to slice the ball. Again use one club longer than normal. Put your weight on the **left** side.

It is very important to take a practice swing when you have an uneven lie. If your practice swing makes good contact with the grass, **Do not change your position**. Kind of scoot up to your ball so you will have the same position as in your practice swing.

Many golfers take a beautiful practice swing and then realign themselves before taking the shot. This makes the first practice swing worthless.

UPHILL/DOWNHILL LIES
On an uphill lie, place the ball about 3" behind your left heel. Use a closed stance and keep your weight on the left side. Aim to the **right** of your target. Hands in front of the ball.

On a downhill lie, place the ball towards the back of your stance with weight on the left side. Use one club more than normal and aim to the **left** of the target. Hands in front of the ball.

On uphill and downhill lies, you want the club head to flow with the landscape of the uneven lie otherwise you will chop the ball.

Take a practice swing as we did on the side hill lies.

~ ~

Two golfers are at the first tee:

Golfer one: ``Hey, guess what! I got a set of golf clubs for my husband!''

Golfer two: ``Great trade!!!!''

~ ~

SUCCESS WITH THE DRIVER

The driver is the most feared and misunderstood club in our golf bag. We put that big thing in our hands and you would think it was a 12 gauge shotgun about to go off all by itself.

Not only does the darn thing look like a monster, but there are always people standing around looking at us. This is one of the few shots in golf where you are on center stage. Let's forget all these dumb thoughts and get to the basics of the tee shot.

There are only **two places** on the golf course that you can legally put your hands on the golf ball. One is on the **tee box** and the other is on **the green** when you putt. All other shots should be played as they lie.

Not only can you put your hands on the ball with the tee shot, but you can place the ball in any position you want within the markers. This is heaven to a good golfer.

Next we have to realize that **every** tee shot is the same no matter what club we use. The only thing that will vary is the distance we have to hit the ball. Our club selection takes care of this decision.

What else could we ask for to make the shot easier? No folks, we can't ask everyone not to watch. We have to have some element to make the shot challenging.

Let's start our lesson with the little wooden tee. For the driver, tee your ball up about 1 1/4 inch above the ground. For the #3 wood, tee it up about 3/4 of an inch above the ground and for the iron shots, tee it up about the height of the top portion of the tee. These heights can vary a bit, but stay close. The oversize club heads can make a difference, so adjust accordingly.

Our next lesson will be to line ourselves up properly. This can be done in several ways. First we have to pick the spot we want to aim for. This is easy because it will be the center of the fairway, right?

Next, we have to line our feet up with our target. Here is our first real challenge. Most golfers try and line up with the middle of the fairway and this **does not** work. Pick a spot about twenty feet in front of your ball. It is much easier to aim for something twenty feet away then 200 yards away.

I like to use divots on the tee box to line my feet up or maybe some brown grass or leaf on the tee box. Anything you can find that is close. Another simple way to line yourself up and this is my favorite, **use the manufactures name** on the ball. Just place the name on the top pointing to your target and then line your feet and the club head up with the name. Simple isn't it?

Address the ball so that it is just about even with your left heel. Use a partially closed stance, (right foot back of target line), and place your weight on the **right** side.

Position your hands **behind** the ball. Line the shaft up close to the middle of your body. The theory here is to hit the ball on the upswing off of the tee.

This will also apply to all other tee shots no matter which club you use. The position of your hands **behind** the ball is the secret here. Almost all other golf shots will have your hands **in front** of the ball.

Now that we are teed up, positioned and aiming in the right direction, we have to hit the darn thing. Here is problem number **ONE**.

The shot gun is about to go off and you are shaking all over. My only advice here is to take a deep breath, relax and just hit the darn thing. It won't hurt.

Now that we got that section out of the way, how about a joke or two?

~~~~~~~~~~~~~~~~~~~~~~~~~~~~~~

Two novice golfers are out on the course one day. The first tees up the ball, swings, and watches as it takes off on a ninety-degree angle. It flies about twenty yards, hits a rock, bounces off a nearby cart path, hits a tree, careens off the tree, and finally comes to rest in the middle of the fairway.

"Hey!" says the friend, giving a miffed look. "Why didn't you tell me you've been practicing?"

~~~~~~

I don't believe in political jokes, I've seen too many of them get elected.

~~~~~~

ELIMINATE THAT SLICE

Over the years I have seen just about every golf shot a person can make. Unfortunately, I have also seen just about everyone slice the golf ball.

My guess would be that about **70 - 80%** of all golfers slice the ball, especially off the tee. How do we eliminate the slice? This chapter will deal with some helpful tips to guide you away from hitting the slice.

In basic terms, the slice is created by striking the golf ball from an outside to inside down swing. The club head comes across the ball from right to left, (reverse for left handers), and puts a **clockwise side spin** on the ball. This clockwise side spin is caught in the air current and sends the ball out to the right.

Since I'm not an engineer, my terminology is probably incorrect, but that is what the ball does.

There are more theories on correcting the slice than there are slicers.

To correct the slice, we have to make **four** simple adjustments. The first is to change your grip. Place the club in your hands as you always do. Now, rotate your hands on the grip to the **right** about **1/4 inch** or so. The V's between your finger and thumb, (on both hands), should be pointing to your right shoulder. This is called a semi **side grip**.

The second adjustment is to stand up a bit straighter and closer to the ball. This will keep you from reaching out to make your swing.

The third adjustment is to use a **closed stance**. This is where your right foot is back of the line parallel to your target. You want to aim to the right of the target. (Reverse for left handed golfers)

Now you say, how come we are making corrections in the same direction (right) as we have been hitting the ball. It is the same theory as driving in the snow. When your car slides right, turn it to the right and it will stop the car from sliding and automatically straighten out your path.

The fourth adjustment is to correct the **swing path** in your back swing and down swing. This is more difficult because you can not see what you're doing back there.

My recommendation is to practice by taking a half back swing and then come down slowly. As you bring the club down to make contact with the ball, **tuck your right elbow into your side** and kind of slide your hips towards your target (shifting your weight). Reducing your **hip turn** a bit will put more hand action into your swing. This will **straighten out** the club face

It is very important to keep the club face aiming toward the target until it can't go any further and then turn the club up and over your shoulder. You have to **really accent this follow through.**

Please do this in **slow motion** without the ball. Stop at the bottom of your swing and look at the club face. If it does not point straight out, then you did not tuck your right elbow into your side enough. This is the most important part of the swing.

The slice will not go away quickly so please stay with it. Once you have corrected the slice, your game will improve **threefold** and your scores will come down.

Again, practice, practice, practice !

PUSHED AND PULLED SHOTS

I receive a lot of letters from people who are pushing the ball out to the right. I also get a lot of letters from people pulling the ball out to the left.

A **pushed** shot is different from a slice in that it does not curve right. It heads to the right from the minute the club face makes contact.

Two things can cause this. One the golfer is lined up to the right and hitting it straight or two: the golfer is gripping the club more on top instead of a semi-side grip where both of the V's, between our thumb and first finger, are pointing to the right shoulder.

To correct the pushed shot I feel it is necessary to be sure you are making a complete body turn and full follow through straight out at your target. If you get lazy and don't complete your turn, you will be hitting the ball as you are facing right and that is where it is going to go.

Next, when you address the ball hold the club in your normal way and then rotate your hands on the grip to the **right** about 1/4". This correction is very similar to correcting the slice.

When you are **pulling** the shot out to the left we make the same adjustment as we did with the push shot only we turn the hands on the grip about 1/4" to the **left**.

We also need to be sure we are in balance, as "falling off" on the left foot will cause the shot to go left.

Always make any new adjustments in small increments until you find the right spot.

THE SHANK SHOT

Now we come to the shank shot which is by far the ugliest shot in golf. Actually it isn't even a golf shot. It is just one big miss hit.

Where does it come from? It is caused by hitting on the club face next to the hosel. The hosel is the part of the club face that connects to the shaft. When this is done the ball goes directly right (reverse for left handers).

OK, now we know what it is, how do we correct it? There is no cure for a shank. It is a complete mental breakdown when swinging the club. Most of the time it happens with a wedge shot around the green. We try and "baby" the ball up onto the green instead of hitting it. By being so careful with the shot, we lean forward, or we lean backwards and do not bring the clubface all of the way through the shot.

We all know better, but we still do it, so how can we come up with a cure? My best guess it to spend more time concentrating on each golf shot we make at all times. If we mentally picture each shot before we swing, we will make better shots and most likely never shank.

~~~~~~~~~~~~~~~~~~~~~~~~~~~~~~~~~~~

"Tell a man there are 300 billion stars in the universe and he'll believe you. Tell him a bench has wet paint on it and he'll have to touch it to be sure."
                                                (Jarger)

~~~~~~~~~~~~~~~~~~~~~~~~~~~~~~~~~~~

THE ART OF PUTTING

More strokes are lost on the putting surface than any other place on the golf course. We will start our putting lesson as we approach the green.

After you have hit upon the green, always walk to your ball from the **other** side of the pin. This way you can see the line of your putt from the opposite direction.

As you walk towards your ball, take a good look at the slope of the green from the pin to your ball. Give it a good look from the side as you pass the pin. If your ball is above the pin, you will have a **fast** putt. If your ball is below the pin, you will have a **slow** putt.

As you walk past the pin you can notice if there is an unusual slope. Now we have analyzed the putt from two different angles. The last look we have will be from behind the ball. We will take that last look in a minute, but first some words of wisdom. The next statement is a very important part of the golf game.

Before we go any further in this putting

lesson we need to get one thing straight. Do not let any player speed up your game.

You paid your green fees and sometimes these can be pretty expensive. You are entitled to play your shots.

You never want to be in the foursome that holds up the whole golf course, but take your time when it is your turn to play. The secret to giving yourself time is to do all of the studying necessary, beforehand, while someone else is playing their shot.

Always be ready to play when your turn comes up, but take the time to play the proper club, the proper stroke and most important, lining up your putt.

DO NOT WORRY ABOUT WHAT THE OTHER PLAYERS THINK.

ALL THEY WANT IS YOUR MONEY.

After you have walked up to your ball from the other side of the pin you are ready to mark it. Be sure the ball is clean and free of dirt particles or sand. While you are cleaning your ball take a good look at the pin from where you stand. This is your final decision on what line you're going to play.

If you see a slight break or slope in the green, you will need to adjust the roll of the ball accordingly. Now, here is one of the secrets of putting. When you place your ball down in front of the marker, place the name of the manufacturer on top and line it up with the spot you are going to use for the putt. If there is a four inch break to the right, line the ball with the manufacturers name four inches to the left of the cup. If the putt is going to be straight, then line the name on the ball straight at the center of the cup, and so on.

Line your feet up with the name on the ball. It is a lot easier to line up with something a few inches away then it is to line up with the hole which may be twenty feet away.

Another thing you can line yourself up with is a mark on the green. There are always some kind of a mark on the green, even if it is a little brown spot, divot or piece of a leaf.

Now that we are lined up we have to stroke the ball. If you are putting downhill, think of your putt as about **half** of the distance. Stroke the putt to a half way point and it will roll the rest of the way all by its self.

If you are putting uphill, stroke the putt to roll **past** the pin. Because it is uphill, it will stop long before you think it should.

When it comes to putting you will hear about "With the Grain", "Against the Grain", "Shinny Surface" and "Dull Surface". **Don't** concern yourself with these things until you have developed a good putting stroke. Let your competitors boggle their minds with this kind of golf jargon.

The putting stance and stroke of the ball is entirely different from all other shots in golf. You stand very close to the ball and kind of hover over it. You keep your head directly over the ball and focus your eyes on the **front edge** of the ball.

I recommend you use arm movement only. Putter head goes straight back and straight forward. **NOTHING ELSE MOVES.**

After you take a practice stroke, you again kind of scoot up to your ball. Do not reset your stance or any thing else.

Almost every putter will have some kind of a line on top of the putter head. Use this line to square the putter face with the ball and line it up directly behind the manufacturer's name. This assures you that you are going to stroke it where you lined up.

As we mentioned earlier, be sure to follow through after stroking the ball. Keep the putter head going straight towards your target until it stops. Keep your wrists, arms and elbows stiff.

When you have a putt of 30 feet, or more, **do not** try and sink it. Think of a three foot ring around the pin and putt to that circle. This will save you from a lot of 3 – 4 putt greens.

You probably weren't paying attention, but I never said hit the golf ball on the green. You **hit** the golf ball on the fairway, and **stroke** the ball on the green.

Always use the same routine for every putt, whether it be twenty feet or three feet. The analysis, the placing of the ball and the lining up of the name on the ball **won't** ever change. If it does, so will your putting score.

This stuff really gets boring so I think it is about time for another joke.

~ ~
~ ~ ~ ~ ~ ~ ~ ~ ~ ~ ~

Son, father and grandfather are playing as a threesome when a beautiful blonde asks to join them.

Obviously they agree and all play the round of their lives.

On the last hole, the blonde has a two-foot putt for her best score ever and promises the best night of sexual passion to any of the three who will help her in making her putt.

The son starts and says, "Smooth stroke, uphill, be firm against the grain."

The father then adds, "Break left 2 inches, play the drop".

Grandpa analyzes the situation and tells the beauty, "Your place or mine? That's a gimme."

~ ~
~ ~ ~ ~ ~ ~ ~ ~ ~ ~ ~

GETTING OUT OF TROUBLE

When I'm out on the golf course, all I see is green pasture land. There are tee makers at one end and a flag pole at the other. There is nothing in between. My playing partners think I'm crazy. All they see are rows of trees, water and sand bunkers all over the place.

I have just received about two strokes from each one of them. When you think trouble, you will find some trouble. No one has ever figured this out, but if you think water, you will hit into the water. If you think sand bunkers you will end up in a sand bunker. Our minds play silly tricks on us.

Now, I have been in a lot of sand bunkers in 70 years and even given my golf ball a bath on numerous occasions, but not 1/3 the times as some of my playing partners. I'm not a better golfer, only I have set my mind on the fact that there is no trouble on a golf course.

Everyone gets into trouble, so, let's talk about our getting **out** of trouble. It is very simple if you take the time to think about it. Haste makes waste and golf shots can be wasted.

TREES

The most common type of problem on a golf course is the tree lined fairways. One, they make the fairways look narrower and two, the ball usually ends up behind one.

Not only does the tree get in your way to the pin, but there are always roots at the bottom of the tree. **Do not** try and go through the trees. Bite the bullet and hit your ball side ways back onto the fairway. This way you only lose one stroke. If you try and go in between the trees on a line to the pin, odds are 7 to 2 that you will hit that tree, another tree, a branch of a tree or even miss the ball entirely on your swing because you are thinking about the darn tree.

When you are in the trees, think **OUT**, not forward.

OK, you are not going to listen to my advice. You are stubborn and want to play between the trees.

Here is the secret. Take your favorite club out of the bag. Hopefully you will choose a 4 iron. Next you place the ball way back in your normal stance and close the club face completely, I mean straight up and down. Using arm movement only with a stiff left elbow, punch the ball out between the trees in line with the pin. Simple isn't it?

SAND

You hit into one of those sand bunkers that I said weren't on the course. OK, so I told a fib. Anyway you are in a sand bunker and feeling sorry for yourself.

Every week I get questions regarding sand bunkers and how to get out of them. My first thought is, don't go into one and you wouldn't have a problem.

Since this won't happen, we shall discuss the proper ways to get out of the sand bunkers, both near and far from the green.

First thing to remember is that you can not ground your club in the sand. There is a one-stroke penalty. The club can not contact the sand until you are completing your down swing to hit the ball.

Green side bunkers: These bunkers are located all around the green. The distance from the green can vary, but normally within 10 yards. Dig your feet into the sand a good two inches so you have solid footing. Because your feet are two inches below the ball, choke up on the cub just a bit to offset that. Use an open stance (left foot back) and open your club face to the sky. Using arm movement only, weight on **left** side, take about a 1/2 back swing and hit the sand **two** inches behind the ball. The most important part of the swing is the **follow through**. Follow through dictates the distance the ball will travel. If you do not follow through, the ball will probably stay in the bunker.

Medium bunker shots: These bunkers are about 40 yards from the green. On these shots you will again dig your feet into the sand about two inches for solid footing. Again, choke up on your club. Your club face should be open just a bit to get the ball up in the air. Take a ¾ back swing and hit the sand about one inch behind the ball. Again, it is important to have a good follow through to get the ball to the green.

Long fairway bunker shots: These bunkers are located out in the fairways, usually in spots that the tee shot might land. This makes for an interesting tee shot and bunker shot. For fairway bunker shots you will again dig your feet into the sand for proper footing. Place the ball in the **middle** of your stance and take a full back swing. You want to hit the ball first on these shots as distance is the most important factor. With these shots you can use a wood or iron depending upon the distance. Again, the follow through is so important to complete the shot.

It rained the night before and the sand bunkers are like hard pan. Play the ball in the middle of your stance. Dig your feet into the hard sand, hit the ball and the sand at the same time. Use arm and hand movement only and **pick** the ball out of the sand. Use a good follow through.

When you are in the sand bunker and there is a big lip between you and the pin, it is recommended that you consider hitting the ball **sideways** and back onto the fairway. This will only cost you one stroke and you are out of the sand bunker. Remember the trees?

WATER

"Water, water everywhere but nary a drop to drink". I think Coleridge wrote that. Well I doubt if he played golf, but he sure knew about water. Some golf courses are like one big lake with a few islands in between with flag poles.

I believe every golfer has fear of water hazards. For some reason, the darn ball just likes to go into water. How do we get around the water fear problem?

My theory is to never see or talk water. It does not exist on the golf course. This may not work for most golfers, so let's take another approach. I've read some interesting theories on hitting over water and I like this one the best.

When you approach a water hole, play to hit **into** it. Now this sounds crazy, but let's analyze the reason for this kind of thinking. If you try and hit your ball into the water what are you actually doing? You are going to hit **down** on the golf ball. What does this do? It pops the ball up in the air and over the water. It really works.

Another good approach is to play your ball so that you plan to hit 110 yards instead of the 75 yards required. This works most of the time, but it is scary. Since I do not see water I don't have the problems that my playing partners have. I just hit a regular shot and it normally goes over the water without any trouble. You may want to consider this simple theory. Just keep your head down and follow through.

TALL GRASS

Pick your club up quickly on the back swing and come down in a chop manner. Hit the ball and the ground about the same time. **Do not** go for distance.

WET GROUND

Always hit the ball first. Try and hit the ball just below the center line. If your club hits the turf first, it will slid into the ball and in effect, top it.

~ ~

"This is the worst golf course I have ever played on." A man said to his caddy during a round of golf one day.

"This isn't the golf course, sir! We left that an hour ago!" The caddy replied.

COURSE MANAGEMENT

This section could be put in with the secrets of the game. What is course management? No, we are not talking about managing a golf course. We are talking about playing smart golf.

As we age and lose our distance, develop aches, lose our eyesight and almost hate the game, there is a way to salvage a score. **Play Smart.**

Playing smart is nothing more than planning our shots and not trying to do things we can't do any more. Here is my secret to low scoring.

I now play to shoot bogey golf. On most courses that comes out to a score of 90. This sounds good to some mature golfers and horrible to many others.

Now, I don't want to shoot 90, but that is the goal I have set for myself every time I go out and play.

This is where course management comes into play. If I try and reach all of the greens in regulation, I would be pushing myself out of control. I would be swinging harder and duffing more shots. My thinking is to reach the greens in one stroke over regulation. That would be three strokes on a four par and four stokes on a five par. This way I am not pushing my self and I swing a lot easier and with a better tempo.

If I play my game and reach the four par's in three, I still have one stroke left to make a par. If I miss the putt than I score a bogey. But I don't score a double bogey. So I saved one stroke, possibly two.

Most four par fairways range between 350 yards up to about 450 yards. If you divide this yardage by three strokes you come out with 133 yards per shot. Don't check my math, I know it is wrong. I picked an average.

Now how many of us can't hit the ball 133 yards? For the lady golfer, the red tees make up for the distance, so you only have to hit the ball about 108 yards to get to the green in three.

Why use a driver, a three wood and a 7 iron if you only have to hit the ball 400 yards on the average? Now you know where course management come in handy. A three wood and two 5 irons will get you there just as easy and you hit those clubs better.

Golf can be put into simple mathematics.

You have to remember that all of your partners are hitting the long ball into the bushes, the trees and every place else, but you are in the middle of the fairway and loving every minute of it.

The hardest part about playing course management is the teasing you will receive from your playing partners. They do not understand the philosophy and just like anything else, they have to make comments. Most of the kidding will be to throw you off your game, but some of them will be very serious.

If you can handle the teasing you will have no trouble staying with your game. After a few rounds they will take notice in what you are trying to accomplish.

Another part of course management is on the putting green. **Do not** try and make those long putts. If you develop a good lag theory and go for two putts, you will be amazed at how many putts you will save.

I figure that if I can play eighteen holes and have around 30 putts, my score will always be in the mid to low 80's. Again we are talking mathematics in golf.

Let's analyze my theory. You will always have one shot off the tee and 2 putts on the green. This leaves two free shots on the fairways (average) to get on the green. No matter how you calculate, this amounts to bogey golf. If you get lucky on your putting that day, then you are in the 80's and whoopee, you shot a good score and relieve your partners of some loose change. I was always told that this is the object of the game.

Not only will you pick up a free drink at the 19th hole, but you will enjoy the game so much more.

Why do full length courses have 18 holes and not 10 or even 20?

During a discussion among the club's membership board at St. Andrews in 1858, one of the members pointed out that it takes exactly 18 shots to polish of a fifth of Scotch. By limiting himself to only one shot of Scotch per hole, the Scot figured a round of golf was finished when the Scotch ran out.

And now you know why we have 18 holes.

~ ~

GOLF EQUIPMENT

This is another game all by itself. Talk about advertising, well these folks in the golf world have to make all sorts of claims to get their share of the market.

I could never understand how every manufacturer's ball goes farther. Someone has to be fibbing. Only one ball can go farther than the others, certainly not all of them.

I will not state any preference as to the best clubs, balls and shoes. They are all good. The only thing we have to think about is what is best for me?

Club "A" feels just great to me, and club "B" seems a bit different. I had better buy club "A" even though club "B" is a better rated club. Fitting clubs to your body and swing tempo is an individual thing and this will never change.

Let me tell you a true story I experienced on the golf course a few years ago. Our twosome was matched up with a single one day. I noticed that the single had the #1 rated set of clubs in his bag. This guy must be some kind of golfer. Well, he only played nine holes and I never saw him hit the ball 150 yards. We got to know each other as the game progressed, and we talked about his clubs. He recently retired and with his bonus check, bought a set of the #2 clubs on the market. He couldn't hit the ball worth a darn, so he gave those to his brother and went out and bought the #1 set of clubs on the market. No matter how you figure his costs, he had to have about $4,000 worth of clubs and he still couldn't hit the ball 150 yards.

What does this tell us? It is not the clubs. It is the person swinging the clubs.

My recommendation for all golfers is to buy the clubs that feel the best to you, regardless of brand name. If you can afford an expensive set of clubs and they fit your swing, buy them. If you are short on funds, then buy the best set for the dollars you have available,

I have been selling used golf clubs for years. I specialize in used clubs for the beginning golfer. I really enjoy working with people and especially new golfers. They haven't the slightest idea what they want, need or should consider.

I do this as a hobby and if I'm lucky, I might pick up some extra pocket change. One thing I do is make sure that the new golfer starts out on the right foot with a set of clubs that fit their needs. All of my clubs are matching sets and in great condition. It is very important to have the irons match. This gives you a constant swing feel and will improve your tempo.

I have written a chapter on buying and cleaning used clubs. It is very interesting. It will be the last chapter in this book.

The manufacturing of clubs has changed over the years. We could go all the way back and start from the beginning, but that would be a whole book by itself. The modern day clubs (1990 - 2013) have changed dramatically in the past 20 years. In the fifties, sixties and seventies we had what they call blade clubs. This is a club head that was pretty much straight up and down. Next came the weighted clubs, where most of the weight was on the bottom of the club. From there they began selling cavity back or perimeter weighted clubs. This technology is still with us today with a variety of metals and club faces.

The perimeter weighted club has a thin inner surface with the weight distributed around the edges. That is where the term "cavity back" came from. Next in the long line of modern technology came the different kinds of club shafts. The most popular being the graphite (light materials) shaft. Next came the different materials used in manufacturing the club heads. We have titanium, tri metal, ten other names and the good old steel head. What ever sells, the manufacturers are making them.

The new technology in manufacturing golf clubs has been a great boom to the golf game. Clubs are lighter, more flexible and the variety of materials fit every golfer's need. This modern technology has improved the distance and scoring in the golf game.

Would Sam Snead and Jack Nicholas out drive Tiger Woods and John Daly? We will never know. Chances are that they would have held their own with these modern clubs.

I am a firm believer that all beginning golfers should buy a used set of clubs. With these clubs they can learn the game of golf. If they don't like the game or just play terrible, they can sell the clubs and not lose a lot of money.

After they have learned the game and decided they want to improve, then they should go out and buy that nice set of clubs.

So darn many people, who take up the game, go out and buy $800 worth of clubs. After about ten tries at the game they decide to quit. Now they are stuck with an expensive set of clubs that no one wants to buy from them. It sure doesn't make sense to me.

How about another joke.

A Golfer sliced the ball from the tee over the hill into a valley. Hearing a yell, he dashed to the top of the hill to see a man lying unconscious below.

When the golfer ran down to the man, the stricken fellow opened one eye and said calmly,
"I'm a lawyer and I'm going to sue you for five thousand dollars."

"I'm sorry", the golfer said, "but I did yell four".

"I'll take it said the lawyer".
~ ~
~ ~ ~ ~ ~ ~ ~ ~ ~ ~ ~

My jokes are not very funny, so let's try two quotes.

"The best vitamin to make a friend: B1"

"The only time the world beats a path to your door is when you are in the bathroom."

Authors are unknown

RULES OF GOLF

The rules of golf are so important. These governing rules make the game fair and competitive. We can't cover the rules of golf in this book because they are too numerous and very complex.

The important thing here is to know that a fair understanding of the rules is mandatory if you are going to play golf.

Understand, right from the beginning, that there are a lot of rule freaks in sports. People who have nothing better to do, will make a lot of noise about rules. These are normally players who do not have a very good game and try to make up for their shortcomings.

The best way to learn the conventional set of rules is ask a friend or someone you know and trust. They can give you some fine pointers on the rules that will keep you out of trouble. We will review some of the main rules below. I can get you from the tee to the green, but after that you are on your own.

The first rule to consider is on the tee box. There will be two colored markers that you must tee your ball between. Place your tee **behind the markers**, and not in front of them. You can tee up within two club lengths behind the markers if you choose. Any other place on the tee is a penalty.

If you hit your ball out of bounds, from the tee or any other place, you will receive a penalty and lose the distance you hit the ball. You will have to hit another ball from the same place as the ball was before you hit it out of bounds. When you hit the next ball, say from the tee, it will be stroke #3. One stroke for the first hit, one stroke for the distance and one stroke for the next shot.

When you get to your ball in the fairway, be sure that ball belongs to you. If you hit someone else's ball there is a penalty. Most golfers place a marking on their golf balls so they can easily identify them.

Do not move or touch your ball in the fairway. There are different local club rules that allow you to move your ball up to six inches in wet conditions. Other than that, there is a penalty.

If you end up behind a new, small tree that is staked, you may move your ball so you will not hit and damage the young tree. There is no penalty. If you end up behind a big tree, too bad and a penalty applies.

There are different markings as you go down the fairway. There are red markings and yellow markings. Ask your friends about this one as it gets into a lot of detail and decisions.

If your ball is in the sand bunker, you may not touch the sand with your golf club. If you do there is a penalty stroke. Take all of your practice swings **outside** of the sand bunker and use a waggle when you approach your shot.

If you hit the flag pole from a shot off the green, congratulations. If you hit the flag pole after your ball is on the green (putting) there is a penalty stroke. Always remove the flag pole while you are putting. Lay the pole some distance from the hole. If you hit it while it is laying down somewhere, there is also a penalty stroke.

There are 1001 rules of golf and maybe more. These I have mentioned above will at least get you down the fairway. After that, good luck.

~ ~
~ ~ ~ ~ ~ ~ ~ ~ ~ ~ ~

"I'm a marvelous housekeeper. Every time I leave a man, I keep his house"

Zsa Zsa Gabor

~ ~
~ ~ ~ ~ ~ ~ ~ ~ ~ ~ ~

GOLF ETIQUETTE

Golf etiquette is the most important thing in golf. If you can't be polite and courteous, you should not be out playing the game.

Talking is one of the biggest offenses. When someone else is taking their shot, **SHUT UP.** Give them the courtesy to concentrate on their shot. The best way to explain golf etiquette is the following:

**"Do unto others as you would
have them do unto you"**

As an example of golf etiquette, let's play down another fairway. This seems to be a good way to explain all of the different parts.

On the tee box, stand back away from the person hitting the ball. Most players stand back 15 - 20 feet or more, to the right or left of the person taking the shot. Do not move around and do not talk. The tee shot is too important to the player at bat.

Always keep your eye on the other person's ball. If they are keeping their head down, as they are suppose to, they may not see the flight of the ball if it does not go straight.

If you are riding in a cart, as most people do, keep the cart on the paved cart paths. Use a 90 degree angle when approaching your ball. This is a courtesy to the golf course and will help keep it in better shape.

When you stop the golf cart at a person's ball, it is normal to pull up about ten feet away and on the ball side of the golfer. This way they know where you are and they don't have to think behind themselves. Some golfers prefer that you park behind them. Let your partner make that decision.

Do not take practice swings while other golfers are making their shot. This is very distracting, just like talking. Do not fiddle with things in the cart or on your golf bag. This is also very distracting. Just stand still. It won't hurt.

When you reach the green, the person closest to the hole should pull the pin. This speeds up the game as they are the last one to putt. This also gives other players a chance to read the putting line without holding up the players behind you.

While on the green, be sure to be aware of where all of the balls are laying. If you see a marker, walk around it. You do not want to walk in the line between the other person's ball and the hole. If your marker will be in the line of another person's putt, they **may** ask you to move your marker. Usually it will be moved about the length of a putter head, maybe two. Pick a tree or some other object and aim your marker for that spot. After the person has made their putt, be sure to remark your ball where it was originally. There is a penalty if you do not put it back in the same spot before it was moved.

When you walk up to a green you may have a couple of clubs in your hand. Always place your clubs, not being used, on the side of the green. It is best to place them in line between the hole and your golf cart. This way you will see them when you leave the green and you will not lose a club.

When someone hits their ball into the bushes or other hazard, do your best to help them find their ball. The rules give you five minutes (maximum) to find a ball. Look for their ball just as hard as you would like them to help you find yours.

If you know a rule of golf that may come up during your round of play, have the courtesy to share it with others if that rule is being tested. This way all golfers can share knowledge in the game of golf and we all will benefit.

PROPER GOLF ATTIRE

Everyone has different ideas of what should be worn on a golf course. In most cases there are no basic requirements or restrictions that golfers have to follow.

As long as you are wearing clothing and have shoes and a shirt, most golf courses will say nothing to their players.

Restrictions come into play when you are playing at a member's golf club or participating in certain events.

Some private and even semi-private courses have simple dress codes.

Shirt Required (with a collar)
Shorts to be a certain length
No Tank Tops or Levis
Golf shoes required
My recommendation to all golfers is to dress comfortably and wear fairly loose fitting clothes.

One thing for certain is you do not want to wear clothing that will inhibit your swinging ability. Fashion has no place on the course if you are serious about your game.

I have seen some golfers come to the course so decked out, they were afraid to move. You may chuckle at this, but it is really true.

Over the years I have played just about every type of course setting and level of society. You wouldn't believe some of the attire that stepped up to the first tee. It sure looked good, but I would want to be on the other team's side when it came to the betting.

Adopting a comfortable dress code depends on where you play. Weather should dictate dress more than your friends.

Speaking of weather, always plan to have the ability to take some clothing off or put it on. You start out at 7:00 in the morning and it is kind of chilly. By 9:00 the jacket and sweater will come off quickly. On the other hand, when you play in the mountains or by the ocean, you will want to add clothing as the day progresses due to the changing weather and winds.

Another point to ponder is the price of clothing. One golf shop will charge you $50 for a nice golf shirt. Down the road, you can buy the same shirt for about $105. I haven't figured this one out yet, but I'm still young.

You may also want to check with your playing partners or phone the course in advance to see what their shoe spike policy is. Some courses are requiring soft spikes on shoes while others do not have requirements.

GOLFERS WITH DISABILITIES

This chapter will not have golf tips. I am not qualified to give advice in this area. I want to take this opportunity to bring to the attention of my readers the current situation facing golfers with disabilities.

There are over 50,000,000 persons with some kind of disability. Of this number there are approximately 9,000,000 persons who are capable of playing the game of golf. So what is the big deal?

The big deal is that most golfing facilities are not set up to accommodate disabled persons. I am not sure what the percentage of golf courses that are set up to welcome the disabled is, but my research indicated less than 1%. That is sad and needs to be addressed.

I have talked to disabled persons about the game of golf. Each has expressed a concern that they are not able to get into the clubhouses, the bathroom facilities are not set up for the handicapped and there are no golf carts for them to ride in and play golf the way their handicap dictates.

The golf courses appear to be taking the stance that there are not enough golfers with disabilities to warrant the added expense of updating their facilities to accommodate them. Well, this creates another problem. The Americans with Disabilities Act, which has been around since the early 1990's, states that all public facilities are required to update their property to accommodate the handicapped person.

So where does this leave us? Right on a path headed for many lawsuits. The golf courses are not going to update facilities until they are forced to comply and the golfer with disabilities is not going to stop wanting to play golf.

The Supreme Court made a ruling in May of 2001 concerning the rights of a disabled golfer to use a golf cart in professional golf tournaments. I am referring to the Casey Martin Decision. Casey Martin is a professional golfer who has a disabling condition that prohibits him from walking long distances without enduring crippling pain.

Casey sued the Professional Golfers Assn. for the right to use a cart when competing in PGA tournaments. After it went through the lower court system, it finally ended up in the land's highest court. Here a decision was made to allow Casey Martin to use the golf cart, referring to the

Americans with Disabilities Act of 1990. Since it did not alter the game of golf as it was intended to be played, he won the case.

The Americans with Disabilities Act is not intended to give disabled persons a benefit that would give them an advantage over the rest of the people. It was intended to give them the opportunity to live a quality life the rest of us enjoy.

How do persons with disabilities play golf? It is amazing what they can do. Without going into detail about the various types of disabilities, we will discuss the equipment that is available to them.

For years, the only equipment available to them was the standard set of golf clubs and the standard golf cart. Over the years special golf clubs were designed to help offset their difficult and uncomfortable swing position, but the golf cart remained standard.

In recent years, new technology has changed the golf cart to accommodate the disabled golfer. Instead of being a regular cart with modifications they now have what is called a single-rider car. These new golf cars are something else. Let me try and describe one.

The one I saw was manufactured by Solo Rider Industries and distributed by Club Car, Inc. It is a work of art.

The car was very modern looking with a sleek design. There was only one seat and this seat does just about anything. It goes up and down, side to side and when those positions don't work it tilts. It tilts forward, backwards and has a 360 degree swivel mechanism.

With all of these positions available to the golfer, they can get themselves into a nearly perfect swing position to hit the ball. There are several straps on the seat to stabilize the golfer and protect the golfer from falling.

The hood of the car has a bag rack so the clubs are conveniently located. The car has hand controls in front of the golfer. Everything is designed with the safety of the golfer in mind. Darn thing even has headlights and a horn.

The best thing about this car is that it is designed to drive on the tee boxes, on the greens, into sand bunkers and not harm the golf course. The secret here is the suspension system. The weight distribution of the car is such that each wheel puts less pressure on the green than a 200 pound person standing on the green. That is unbelievable.

Are there any special rules for the disabled golfer? Not really. It is my understanding that all of the rules of golf apply to their round as well as mine. I do believe that when a condition on the golf course might jeopardize the safety of a disabled golfer, certain rules are implemented for safety purposes. Two that come to mind are sand bunkers and side hill lies.

In sand bunkers the golfer has a choice. They can play the ball as it lies, move the ball to the edge of the sand where the ball is in the bunker, but the cart is on the fairway, or take a penalty stroke and remove the ball from the sand bunker, no closer to the pin.

Another instance where the rules may be a bit different is when the ball is lying on the side of a hill and the golfer may feel unsafe swinging at such an angle.. The golfer may take a shot from where it lies or move it to a more level area, no closer to the hole.

There may be more instances where the disabled golfer can move the ball, but these are the two main ones regarding safety.

What kind of scores do golfers with disabilities shoot? Believe it or not, many are single digit handicappers. The average disabled golfer doesn't shoot low scores. They are just grateful and happy to be out on the course with the rest of us.

I used to live on a golf course. My patio was located about 20 yards from the 6th tee. It was a

180 yard par three. There were two handicapped golfers playing the course at least once a week. They did not play together, but I always noticed them and made conversation whenever possible.

One golfer had been playing for about two years while the other was just starting to learn the game under his new circumstances. Neither had a special cart, they played from their wheelchairs. Golfer #1 was hitting the ball about 75 yards when I first saw him and #2 golfer was getting maybe 30 yards.

When I moved several years later, I saw the #1 golfer almost get the ball on the green. The #2 golfer had improved his tee shot to about 90 yards. I was so happy for the both of them. They were not going to let that wheelchair hold them back. What could these two golfers do if they had one of the modern single-rider cars?

I asked a disabled friend of mine in Arizona what kind of experiences he had playing golf, from a cart, when it came to other golfers. He said most people are very happy to see him out there. When he is playing slow, he lets them play through. When he is riding on the green, most people understand, but he has been turned in to the pro shop on more occasions then he wants to admit. People just don't understand the situation.

What does the golfer with disabilities face in the future? I don't really know. I'm in hope that all golf courses will comply with the Disabilities Act, but I'm sure there will many lawsuits filed against courses that refuse to make improvements until they are sued.

This is America and sometimes we do things the hard way, but we always seem to pull ourselves up by the bootstraps and do things the right way.

So my friends, when you see a golfer out on the course in a wheelchair, in a modified scooter or even one of the new single-rider cars, wish them the very best and think to yourself:

"May the Golf Gods smile upon them,"
"May they always hit the fairways"

GOLFING FOR JUNIORS

Oh, the world of junior golfing. What a great way for your kids to learn the sport.

Junior golfing organizations have been around for years, but not until Tiger Woods appeared in the golf world, have they been so popular. He has done wonders for the game of golf and especially for the junior golfer.

What is the best way to teach your kids the game of golf? There are many theories on the subject and most of them are correct.

Let me use the next few pages of this book to express my views on the subject.

When I was four years old, my dad cut down an old wood shafted 7 iron for me. All he told me was **do not** tear up the course. After that I was on my own. I played on the fairway in front of our summer cabin every night until the golf maintenance crew came by and kicked me off. As soon as they left I would be right back out there.

I never learned how to properly hold the club or swing the darn thing, but I could sure hit that 7 iron. Even today, 70 years later, the 7 iron is my favorite club.

What kind of golf game would I have today if only I had the opportunity to join a junior golf program? We will never know.

I am a firm believer that all junior golfers should have proper instruction. But, before the instruction starts, I also believe that all junior golfers should have the opportunity to get out there and swing the club anyway they can.

Why do I say this? Let them develop their own swing tempo. It will start out too fast and they will try and kill the ball every time they swing. This is OK even though it will hurt **YOU** every time you see them take a whack at the ball.

Take the kids to a driving range. Teach them the proper way to hold the club and the proper stance to address the ball. After that let them go at it.

After some time at the driving range, take the kids out on a golf course and let them feel the experience of being into the game. They will drive you nuts, but that is OK. They are learning.

Before you take the kids out on the course, be sure to teach them proper etiquette and respect of the golf course itself. These two lessons are very important.

After the kids have been to the driving range several times and had a chance to play on a real golf course, you will find them very tuned into getting golf lessons. They will be ready to accept instruction and improve upon their game. It takes time for young children to figure out that just hitting a golf ball is not going to work. There has to be more to golf than that. By now they have the golf bug and in their own minds are ready to learn the proper way.

Now they are ready to join a junior golf group and the instruction they receive will sink in so much easier.

Junior golf groups vary upon economic conditions and locations of the participants. All of the programs are supervised by professionals and the instruction is based on three levels of golf. The beginning junior, the intermediate junior and the advanced junior.

Some of the clinics are free while others charge a small fee to cover costs. These clinics will be held at a driving range either on a golf course or at a special location.

Instruction includes:

1) Gripping the club
2) Proper stance
3) Swing path and tempo
4) Back swing and follow through
5) Putting
6) Golf rules
7) Golf etiquette
8) Respect of the golf course
9) Tournament play
10) And much more

Some junior golf clinics have tournaments between the junior golfers and sometimes a tournament with their parents. They make it very interesting for the children.

You read so much now a days about parents getting over involved with their child's sports and make it very hard for the teachers and other parents officiating. **DO NOT** let this happen in junior golf. These instructors are professionals and know what they are doing. Just stand back and let them do their thing. Trust me, it won't hurt.

~ ~

Things that irritate a sane person

"You can never put anything back in a box the way it came."

"Your tire gauge lets out half of the air while you are trying to get a reading."

"You have to try on a pair of sunglasses with that stupid little plastic thing in the middle of them."
Authors unknown

~~~~~~~~~~~~~~~~~~~~~~~~~~~~~
~~~~~~~~~~~

A LITTLE GOLF HUMOR

Every book I write has to have some kind of jokes, quotes or cartoons. Normally I place them in the body of the book, so I can keep my readers awake.

For some reason I changed my plan and decided to put most of them in a separate chapter at the end of the serious stuff. If you fell asleep while reading my book, I hope you had some good dreams.

Par on #1, Birdie on #2, Chip in on #3, etc..

These are jokes that can be told in mixed company. I picked the following because they are kind of neutral and not the usual ones you will hear on the golf course.

If you've heard them before, laugh anyway.
A good laugh never hurt anyone.

OK, HERE WE GO

~~~~~~~~~~~~~~~~~~~~~~~~~~~~~~~~~~

A man and his wife were celebrating their 30th wedding anniversary with a round of golf. On the first tee, the man told his wife that he had a confession to make, "Honey, fifteen years ago I had an affair with my secretary."

His wife was a little shocked, but now it was her turn. "Darling, I also have a confession to make. One year before we were married, I had a sex change operation!"

With a look of total disgust the husband replied, "And you've had the nerve to play off the lady's tees all these years?"

~~~~~~~~~~~~~~~~~~~~~~~~~~~~~~~~~~

A fellow goes to the doctor and says, "I'm really worried about my wife. I ask her a question and she never answers. I think she's going deaf."

"That's possible," answers the doctor. "But in order to help, we'll have to determine the extent of her hearing problem. I suggest that you run a little test to see how bad the problem really is."

At that point the doctor gave him instructions. The next day the two are out on the golf course. She's plum bobbing a putt, and he steps 15 feet away from her and asks, "Which way do you think it will break?"

No answer.

He steps 5 feet closer and asks the same question, and still no answer.

Again 5 feet closer, and again still no answer. Finally he moves to within inches of her ear and asks, "Which way do you think it will break?"

She snaps, "For the **fourth** and final time, I think the damn thing breaks to the left!"

~~~~~~~~~~~~~~~~~~~~~~~~~~~~~~~~~

Over the loud speaker at the golf course, the starter in the pro shop blurted out, "Would the gentleman on the ladies tee box please back up to the men's tee"

Nothing happened, so he came back on the speaker, and in a louder voice.

"Would the gentleman on the ladies tee box PLEASE back up to the men's tee."

The guy on the ladies tee threw his club down on the ground, turned around and yelled back to the Pro shop.

"Would you please shut up so I can take my second shot."

~~~~~~~~~~~~~~~~~~~~~~~~~~~~~~~

A man was sitting in his dentist's chair, when the dentist asked him to scream
loudly as if he were in great pain.

He asked, "Why? I'm not in any pain."

The dentist replied, "There are too many people in the waiting room, and I have a 2 o'clock tee time."

~~~~~~~~~~~~~~~~~~~~~~~~~~~~~~~

In primitive society, when native tribes beat the ground with clubs and yelled, it was called witchcraft; today, in civilized society it is called golf.

Golf is an expensive way of playing marbles.

Golf is a game in which the slowest people in the world are in front of you, and the fastest people are those behind you.

There is no game like golf: you go out with three friends, play eighteen holes, and return with three enemies.

Many a golfer prefers a golf cart to a caddy because the cart cannot count, criticize or laugh.

Bill was having a really bad day on the golf course. Right around the 14th hole, it seems he had missed one putt too many. He let loose of a fairly impressive string of some profanities, grabbed his putter, and stormed off toward the lake by the 15th tee.

"Uh-oh," said his caddie to one of the playing partners, "There goes that club."

"You think so?" said the golfer. "I've got five bucks says he misses the water!"

A foursome consisting of 3 young players and an old man were getting ready to putt on the green.

The devil decided he wanted to get into some mischief, so he appeared suddenly on the green, halfway between the players and the flag stick.

The three young players screamed in a panic, and then took off. The old man stayed over his putt, lining it up. The devil was confused by the old man's courage.

"Don't you know who I am?" said the devil.

"Sure do", said the old man.

"Aren't you afraid?" asked the devil.

"Nope".

"Why not?" asked the devil, still confused.

"Because I have been married to your sister for over 45 years now!"

~~~~~~~~~~~~~~~~~~~~~~~~~~~~~~~~~

Reasons Why Golf Is Better Than Sex

You don't have to sneak your golf magazines into the house.

If you are having trouble with golf, it is perfectly acceptable to pay a professional to show you how to improve your technique.

The Ten Commandments don't say anything about golf.

If your partner takes pictures or videotapes of you golfing, you don't have to worry about them showing up on the Internet when you become famous.

Your golf partner won't keep asking questions about other partners you've golfed with.
It's perfectly respectable to golf with a total stranger.

When you see a really good golfer, you don't have to feel guilty about imagining the two of you golfing together.

If your regular golf partner isn't available, he/she won't object if you golf with someone else.

When dealing with a golf pro, you never have to wonder if they are really an undercover cop.

You don't have to go to a sleazy shop in a seedy neighborhood to buy golf stuff.

You can have a golf calendar on your wall at the office, tell golf jokes and invite coworkers to golf with you without getting sued for harassment.

If you want to watch golf on television, you don't have to subscribe to a premium cable channel.

Nobody expects you to promise to golf with just one partner for the rest of your life.

Nobody expects you to give up golfing if your partner loses interest in the game.

You don't have to be a newlywed to plan a vacation primarily for the enjoyment of golf.

Your golf partner will never say, "What? We just golfed last week! Is that all you ever think about?"

~ ~

Arnold Palmer is playing in a big tournament and comes to a par 3 which measures 235 yards. After some deliberation, he takes out his 3 iron and sails the ball 20 feet over the pin and backs it up to within 3 feet of the pin.
A fan in the crowd said "Mr. Palmer, how do you make a 3 iron back up like that?"

Mr. Palmer replied, "Do you own a 3 iron?"

The fan said, "Yes, sir I do."

"How far do you hit it?" said Palmer.

"About 160 yards" was his reply.

Palmer calmly said, "What the hell do you want it to back up for?"

THE ART OF CLEANING OLD GOLF CLUBS

Copyright © by Carey Erichson 2003

The following are excerpts from several magazine articles I have written regarding used golf clubs.

Most of the material is very useful and can be a great savings when buying the children or grandchildren some golf clubs.

There are only two conditions of golf clubs that can not be cleaned. One is a very pitted surface and the other is a club that the outer surface has been chipped or scraped off. These two conditions normally come on clubs that were left in extreme moisture or fiercely banged around.

A third condition that is common among older clubs is discoloration. This is a combination of moisture and just plain old age. The clubs can be cleaned, but will not look as good as others.

Other than the examples mentioned above, I have been able to clean, polish and resell almost every club I purchased. Before we get into the subject of cleaning, let's talk a little about purchasing old clubs. Most of the sets we purchase come from garage sales and thrift stores.

They are dirty, dusty, rusty and some have cobwebs. The sellers are not interested in making them look good. Their goal is to resell them or clean out the garage. The prices will vary from .50 to 2.00 per club or maybe $15 to $35 for a set with a bag that should be in the garbage can.

When buying a set of old clubs, always be sure that the irons are of the same make and model. This is important due to the swing weight of the clubs. You can have a different set of woods, but again be sure the older woods are of the same make and model. In today's world of golf, modern technology lets us have different metal woods, but we still need to have matching irons.

Secrets to buying old golf clubs:

Iron Purchases

Look for pits and chipped surfaces mentioned above.

Hold the club by the grip and look down the shaft to see if it is bent and if the club head is in proper position.

Check the grips to be sure they are not torn or ripped. Some of the grips will be smoother than others. These can be brushed up or regripped depending on how much money you want to spend. If they are torn at the
bottom of the grip you can use a knife and cut off the very lower end and wrap with electrical tape to form a cap.

Don't be afraid of rust or some other kind of discoloration. Our cleaning process will correct this.

The most important thing is to have a good surface on the face. The grooves should be deep and not all marred.

Wood Purchases

Same checks as 1-3 above. The most important thing in woods is a good hitting surface. Some older woods have wood faces while others have a plastic face. Be sure there are no cracks on the face and that the grooves are not all nicked up.

The weakest point on a wood is the joint between the shaft and the club head. This area will not break, but the coating material covering the joint will get chipped, cracked or the binding will become loose and unravel. An experienced club man can rewrap the bindings or glue the coating material. The average person should stay clear of this situation. It could be a deeper problem than the surface shows.

Examine the bottom of the wood head. There will be a metal plate on the bottom with inset screws. Check to be sure the screws are in place and secure. There should be no splits in the wood on any part of the club head (bottom or top). Nicks are OK.

Nine irons, pitching wedges and putters will be the rusty clubs because they are left on the grass around the green. These will also be the hardest to clean.

When buying an old bag, be sure all the zippers work. Nylon is the hardest material to clean because it streaks. Vinyl bags can be cleaned up nicely. Many old bags will be missing carrying straps. If the bag is in good condition, you can buy a strap for about $3.00.

The inside of the bag may be missing the club separators or they could be broken. You can purchase a 3/4 inch leather belt at a thrift shop for about $1. Feed the belt through the slots in the top side of the bag and you have separators.

With older clubs' a starter set consists of #3-5-7-9 irons, putter and #1 & #3 woods.

Full sets consists of #3 thru #9 irons, putter and #1 & #3 Woods. If you find a set with a #5 wood or maybe a pitching wedge, you have a good buy.

Now that you are an expert in purchasing old clubs, let's discuss what we can do with them. Although I am basically a salesman, I really get excited when I make a good buy. Nothing is better than going to a garage sale and finding a perfect set of clubs and bag for $35.00. Well, this happens about one in 50 purchases so I had to learn, (the hard way), to get the old clubs in shape. Here is where I'm going to surprise you with simplicity.

The first thing we need you to do is get the proper cleaning tools. Like I said in my introduction letter, the process is very economical. Here is all you need:

1) Any cheap laundry detergent you have around the house. It must be the old, real cheap, powder type.

2) An S.O.S. pad. **Do not** substitute with any other brand.

3) A small wire brush. The best type is with brass bristles.

4) An old towel. You will get rust on it and the lady of the house won't get upset.

5) A kitchen sink with running hot & cold water. THAT'S IT!!

Phase one of the cleaning process is to soak the irons in very hot water with lots of laundry soap. **DO NOT** put the wood clubs in the hot water with laundry soap. It will peel off the surface and warp the club head. We will clean the woods later. Let the irons soak for as long as the water is still hot. Probably one hour.

While the irons are soaking, take your woods and get them wet in the soapy water. With your wire brush, scrape out the grooves on the club face. Don't be afraid to put some pressure on the brush, you will not damage the club. If there is paint in the grooves, don't scrub so hard as to take it off. The manufacturers coat the painted surfaces very well and it looks nice. After you have cleaned the club face, scrub the bottom plate and get all the junk off. It could be grass stain or some other substance. The wire brush will take most of it off by using a circular motion.

Now take your S.O.S. pad and get it wet and soapy. Clean the club head, top and bottom. The S.O.S pad will not damage the surface of the club head. Don't scrub as hard as you do with the brush, but give it a little authority. After you have cleaned the club head, take the wire brush and scrub the metal shaft. If it is not rusty or messed up, then just use your S.O.S pad and clean it good. Rinse off the entire club with warm water and dry. We will return to the woods later.

After you have finished with the wood clubs, take a break until the irons have soaked for a while.

When the irons are ready to clean, you will again start out with the wire brush. This time you will probably have to scrub a little harder than you did with the woods. You can not hurt the metal surfaces as long as you use common sense. Take the brush and clean the grooves. You will always find rust in the hosel of the club face. That is where the face ends and curves up to the shaft. Scrub back and forth, sideways and up and down, what ever it takes to get firm pressure on the surface. Sometimes the rust is in a place that the brush just seems to miss, so keep on trying. It will come off!!

With the wire brush, scrub the bottom of the club. Sometimes you will see streaks on the bottom. This is just like the metal plate on the woods. These are grass stains or some other substance. This will be one area where there will be scratches that may not come out. You can get the area clean, but the deep scratches are there to stay. Next scrub the back of the club and then go to the shaft. If the shaft is not really rusty, then leave it alone. The S.O.S. pad will get it clean.

The next trick is to clean the club with the S.O.S. pad. Scrub the iron head and shaft. Next dip the club grip in the soapy water and give it a good cleaning with the S.O.S pad. Many times you will find that the slick surface on the grip area is a build up of dirt and hand grease. If you clean it good with the S.O.S pad you will notice a difference. If it is still smooth, take the wire brush and ruff up the grip. Dry the club and shaft right after you finish. After you have cleaned all of the clubs, clean up your mess in the kitchen so it will be nice and neat.

Now that you have cleaned the clubs it is time to make them look nice. This is the fun part. There is not much you can do to the irons. Once they are clean, that's it, but the woods are another story. Many times there will be nicks in the wood heads, and/or the bottom will be worn from wear and tear.

Take some shoe polish and shine the club heads. If the nicks are deep, you can get one of those marker pens and fill in the worn spots. Be careful not to color any writing on the club head. This will normally be a pro's name or club marking. This was put there for a purpose and you don't want to cover up any identification as to the value of the club. A signature club is always worth more than a plain old, no name club. Use plain old shoe polish for shining the club head. After you apply the shoe polish, brush the club and use a shine cloth. The wood head will sparkle. The next trick is to apply furniture polish on the wood head. This really makes the club head shine and it will also smell good. (Now a good smelling club head will really improve your golf game.)

As a bonus feature, I will now tell you how you can pick up some extra money. Since you are now a pro at cleaning clubs you might as well make some money in the golf club business. Not only is it a fun pastime, but it can also be very profitable.

Go to a few garage sales and/or thrift shops and find some old golf clubs. You do not want to pay more than $15 - $25 for a starter set and $25 - $35 for a full set of clubs. Take the clubs home and get them nice and clean. Then tell your friends or coworkers that you have a set of clubs for sale. Your selling price is $45 for the starter set and $65 for the full set. This will be the best price in town for an all matching, clean set of clubs. I buy golf bags and sell them separately for $10 to $15 depending on the condition and the number of pockets on the bag. You do not have to sell the clubs and bags together. It is more profitable to sell them separate.

I do all of the selling out of my home. I have built my business up to about 10 sets of clubs a month and this adds up to a nice piece of change, and I enjoy the work. Because my clubs are all matching, very clean and reasonable in price, I have developed a nice referral service so people are now calling me for clubs.

I hope this pamphlet has been informative for you and will help you get those old clubs clean. The process does work and if you become involved in the cleaning of clubs you will find out over a period of time that there are tricks of the trade that have to be learned on your own. Just remember that the basics will not change so if you start there, you're on your way!!

SUMMARY OF GOLF SHOTS

Below we will list, in outline form, the correct approach to hitting all of the different shots. You can tear this section out of the book and put it in your golf bag.

THE DRIVE
Partially closed stance
Weight on right side
Ball even with left heel
Hands behind ball
Align body to right of target

FAIRWAY WOODS
Square Stance
Weight on left side
Ball inside left heel
Hands in front of ball
Align to right of target

LONG IRONS
Square Stance
Weight on left side
Ball in middle of stance
Hands in front of ball

SHORT IRONS
Open stance
Weight on left side
Ball towards right foot
Hands in front of ball

WEDGES
Open stance
Open club face
Arm & hand shot only
Weight on left side
Hit ball crisply
Feet closer together

SAND SHOTS
Open stance
Open club face
Arm & hand shot only
Weight on left side
Hit 2" behind ball
Feet in medium position

UPHILL LIES
Closed stance
Weight on left side

DOWNHILL LIES
Medium open stance
Weight on left side

Ball towards left heel
Aim to right of target
Open club face more

Ball towards right heel
Aim to left of target
Use one club longer

SIDE HILL LIES

FEET BELOW BALL
Closed stance
Ball middle of stance
Take Practice swing
Then scoot up to ball
Choke up on club
Aim to right of target
Weight on left side

FEET ABOVE BALL
Open stance
Ball towards left foot
Take practice swing
Then scoot up to ball
Use one club longer
Aim to left of target
Weight on left side

PUTTING
Approach ball from opposite side of pin to check line
Walk past pin looking for slopes and angles
Take a good look at line from behind ball. (Final Decision)
Your first impression is normally the correct one
Do not over read a putt
Mark Ball, lift and clean
Replace ball with manufacturer's name facing line of putt
Head and eyes directly over ball, Focus on front edge of ball
Take a practice swing, then scoot up to your ball
Line up center marking on putter head with line of putt
Arm movement only
Keep wrist and elbows stiff
Follow through direct at target
Extend follow through until putter has to stop

CLUB YARDAGE CHARTS

Based on National Averages

CLUB	**MEN**	**WOMEN**
Driver	210 yards plus	180 yards plus
3 Wood	190 yards plus	165 yards plus
5 Wood	170 yards	150 yards
3 Iron	175 yards	150 yards
4 Iron	165 yards	140 yards
5 Iron	155 yards	130 yards
6 Iron	145 yards	120 yards
7 Iron	135 yards	110 yards
8 Iron	125 yards	100 yards
9 Iron	115 yards	90 yards

Wedges vary with each shot

You can figure just about 10 yards difference in each club.

Yardage will vary with size and age of golfer.

CAREY ERICHSON PUBLICATIONS
1-800-717-4633

Fairy Tales From The I.R.S.
(You won't believe what they can do to you)

Business is a Bitch
(Wonders of the business world)

Willie Learns A Lesson
(The Story Of A Naughty Little Fish)

The Rise and Fall of American Family Values
(What is happening to America)

Cohabitate or Remarry
(The Possible Pitfall of Remarrying)

The Golf Shot Maker
(Details every golf shot on the course)

Our Joke Book Series

I Laughed so hard I Peed My Panties
OOOpppss I Peed MY Panties Again
Daddy's Dirty Little Black Book
The Book Of Risque' Jokes
Mommy Dirty Little Secrets
The Day My Private Part Died
Where Did My Willie Go
Where Did My Virginity go
GrandPa's Naughty Joke book
GrandMa's Naughty Naughty Joke Book

Risque' Jokes Unlimited

PLEASE VISIT OUR WEBSITE

Kartines.com

**Golf Products
Bowling Products
Products For The Disabled
NFL Football
Books**

Made in United States
Orlando, FL
01 December 2023